Visit us on the Web! rhcbooks.com

Educators and librarians, for a variety of teaching tools, visit us at RHTeachersLibrarians.com

*Library of Congress Cataloging-in-Publication Data*
Names: Gilland, Åsa, illustrator.
Title: Welcome to California / by Åsa Gilland.
Description: First edition. | New York : Doubleday, [2021] | Audience: Ages 3–7. |
Summary: "An illustrated introduction to the state of California" —Provided by publisher.
Identifiers: LCCN 2020010019 (print) | LCCN 2020010020 (ebook)
ISBN 978-0-593-17823-2 (trade) | ISBN 978-0-593-17824-9 (ebook)
Subjects: LCSH: California—Juvenile literature.
Classification: LCC F861.3 .G55 2021 (print) | LCC F861.3 (ebook) | DDC 979.4—dc23

MANUFACTURED IN CHINA
10 9 8 7 6 5 4 3 2 1
First Edition

# WELCOME to CALIFORNIA

illustrated by **Åsa Gilland**

Doubleday Books for Young Readers

WELCOME to CALIFORNIA!

WE'RE GLAD YOU'RE HERE!

ALASKA

WASHINGTON
OREGON
CALIFORNIA
SACRAMENTO
NEVADA
IDAHO
MONTANA
WYOMING
UTAH
ARIZONA
NEW MEXICO
COLORADO
NORTH DAKOTA
SOUTH DAKOTA
NEBRASKA
KANSAS
OKLAHOMA
TEXAS
MINNESOTA
IOWA
MISSOURI
ARKANSAS
LOUISIANA
WISCONSIN
ILLINOIS
INDIANA
MICHIGAN
OHIO
KENTUCKY
TENNESSEE
MISSISSIPPI
ALABAMA
GEORGIA
PENN
WEST VIRGINIA
NORTH CAROL
SOUTH CAROL
FLORID

HAWAII

CALIFORNIA REPUBLIC

MAINE
NEW HAMPSHIRE
VERMONT
MASSACHUSETTS
RHODE ISLAND
CONNECTICUT
NEW JERSEY
DELAWARE
MARYLAND

Capital city: Sacramento
State nickname: The Golden State
State motto: "Eureka"

Hot deserts, snowy mountaintops, lush farms, giant forests, and the huge waves of the Pacific Ocean—California has it all! It is the third-largest state in the USA.

# CALIFORNIA

CRESCENT CITY

ALTURAS

EUREKA

SACRAMENTO

NAPA

SAN FRANCISCO

SANTA CRUZ

BIG SUR

SUN, SAND & BEACH

THE PACIFIC OCEAN

LAKE TAHOE

YOSEMITE NATIONAL PARK

SEQUOIA NATIONAL FOREST

DEATH VALLEY

FRESNO

RIDGECREST

JOSHUA TREE NATIONAL PARK

SAN LUIS OBISPO

PALM SPRINGS

SANTA BARBARA

LOS ANGELES

SANTA ANA

SAN DIEGO

The state bird of California is the California quail. It has a curved feather that sticks up from its forehead like a ponytail!

CALIFORNIA POPPY

The California poppy is the state flower. Poppies can keep themselves warm by closing up their petals, like a tiny hug.

CALIFORNIA GRIZZLY BEAR

GRANDPA ~ CALIFORNIA, 1920

There are no California grizzly bears anymore, but this huge creature is still the state animal.

Other kinds of grizzly bears live in the United States, and we must protect them so they will live long into the future.

The biggest trees you'll ever see are in California!
The redwood tree is the tallest living thing on Earth.

The redwood forests are important! They are home to animals such as mountain lions, coyotes, and bobcats. And trees make oxygen, which keeps the air clean to breathe.

California has big cities, too. San Francisco is a city full of steep hills. But if you get tired climbing them, hop on a cable car to take you up and down!

You can also see the Golden Gate Bridge in San Francisco.
It was once the longest suspension bridge in the world.

California is full of yummy food, thanks to its immigrants from countries such as Mexico, China, Japan, and Italy. Sunny California also has lots of farms and grows delicious fruits and vegetables.

ARTICHOKES

GRAPES

TACOS

AVOCADOS

TOMATOES

TACOS

SUSHI

STRAWBERRIES

DUMPLINGS

FORTUNE COOKIES

CIOPPINO

BURRITOS

WHICH one is your FAVORITE?

How would you like to hop on a skateboard and whiz around a skate park? Or surf the big waves of the Pacific Ocean? You can! Sun's out, surf's up!

Do you like to watch movies and TV shows? Lots of them are made in Hollywood. You might see a famous actor or actress—and you can put your hands and feet in their prints in the sidewalk!

A big place like California has a lot of unusual things to see if you're out for a drive:

# LA BREA TAR PITS

Can you imagine giant prehistoric animals, such as mammoths and saber-toothed cats, roaming downtown Los Angeles? They once lived on that land, and now you can see their fossils at the La Brea Tar Pits. The bones of these creatures were found in the sticky oil that still bubbles up from the ground.

# BUBBLEGUM ALLEY

Chomp, chew . . . ewww! There's a place in San Luis Obispo called Bubblegum Alley, where visitors stick their used chewing gum on the walls!

# GIANT LEMON

This huge lemon was built for a Fourth of July parade in 1928, and it now sits in Lemon Grove, a town famous for growing this very sour fruit.

If you love California, then you're a California kid!
And California kids are the best!

UNITED STATES AME